T0129522

FORGIVE TO PROSPER

VICTIM NO MORE: LIVE A BOUNTIFUL LIFE

A 40-DAY *INTENTIONAL* FORGIVENESS PRACTICE WORKBOOK

W. L. WATSON WILFONG

WestBow
PRESS
A DIVISION OF THOMAS NELSON

Copyright © 2011 W. L. Watson Wilfong, R.Sc.P

All rights reserved. No part of this book may be used or reproduced by any means, graphic, electronic, or mechanical, including photocopying, recording, taping or by any information storage retrieval system without the written permission of the publisher except in the case of brief quotations embodied in critical articles and reviews.

WestBow Press books may be ordered through booksellers or by contacting:

WestBow Press
A Division of Thomas Nelson
1663 Liberty Drive
Bloomington, IN 47403
www.westbowpress.com
1-(866) 928-1240

Because of the dynamic nature of the Internet, any web addresses or links contained in this book may have changed since publication and may no longer be valid. The views expressed in this work are solely those of the author and do not necessarily reflect the views of the publisher, and the publisher hereby disclaims any responsibility for them.

Any people depicted in stock imagery provided by Thinkstock are models, and such images are being used for illustrative purposes only.

Certain stock imagery © Thinkstock.

ISBN: 978-1-4497-2093-3 (sc)
ISBN: 978-1-4497-2094-0 (e)

Library of Congress Control Number: 2011911729

Printed in the United States of America

WestBow Press rev. date: 10/27/2011

To my children and their children and my entire family and hosts of friends: Whenever you feel as a victim, forgive and then you will be a victim no more – you will be free.

Contents

APPRECIATION AND GRATITUDE LIST

It's with an appreciative and grateful heart that I acknowledge those
who through the years or just a moment's encounter effected me with
pure inspirations, insights, conflicts, and lessons learned.

A Course in Miracles Study Group
(Maryland/Washington DC)
Adeyemi, Ngozi, Ama, Nsia, Jingles, Papaya,
Marjorie, Freddy, Ravell and Winnie, Mushinda,
Janice, Kathy, Kwasi, Elise and Terry
Acts of Power Transformational Organization
Adama, Bobba, Kweli, Sika, Babu
Agape International Spiritual Center Family
Agape Internt'l Spiritual Center Ministerial Staff
Agape Practitioner Class of 1992
Rev. Ahman
Dr. Akmal Muwwakkil
Charles Allen-Anderson
Cousin Alice
Carl Anderson (d)
Anthony Robinson, Esq.
Jeanne Alexander
Lola Alexander
Allohn
Antolina
The Arius Group
Bob Armstead
David Askew
Aqebi
Jean-Claude and Arlene Audergon, Ph.D.
Nassoma Bahati
The Baileys
Jerome Bailey
The Baltimore folks
Barry (d), Billy, Landry (d), Michael, Teddy
Edna Battey and family
Akili G.F. Beckwith, R.Sc.P.
Celeste Beckwith, R.Sc.P.
The Rev. Michael Bernard Beckwith
Rickie Byars Beckwith and the Agape International
Choir
The entire Beckwith Family
Cal and La Donna Bennett
Stanley and Chemin Bernard
Bill and Bonnie Birkhofer
Aunt Bessie C. Watson Black (d)
Rickey, Constance, Craig, Mary, David, Elena Black
and Families
Harmony Blair
Jimmy Bond
The Boston friends and Family
The Boudreaux – Chris and Karen (d) Family
Rev. Audrey Bowen
Dave Bradfield and Patricia A. Watson Bradfield,
Sharry, Christy and Family
Terry Bradford
Marcia Bradshaw
Sybil Brand L.A.Cty Facility coworkers and inmates
Lisa Braun
Angela Brown – Doula Love's Creation
Grayvette Brown and James Brown
Medea Brown
Royce Tarleeb Brown
Sesheta Brown
Thelma Brown
Marcie, Wayne and Joey Bruce
The Brundidge Family
The Pasadena Bryants
Sam, Heather, Sydney and Morgan Bryant
Misumbo Byrd

B J Cahill
Ramona IAM Carter
Janvie Cason
Celebration Center for Spiritual Living Family and
Practitioners
The Center (Waller) Family
Mr. Chuck Chance
Rev. Arthur Chang
Circle of Light
Tommy Cobb
Barbara Jean Watson Coleman (d) and Herbert
Coleman (d) and Mallory, Lynn and Darryl, Kim and
Kim and Bradford
Aunt Corrine
Bea Curl, R.Sc.P.
Cuz (d)
Kelly Vaughn-Davis
Damion A. Davis
Stanley (Monte) Davis, Timothy, D'Shawn, Bret,
Shahalazard and Marianne
Janice Deverman
Robin Diakhate
The Divine Order of Guidance Practitioners
The Drisdoms
Delightful Deborah Ducre'
Brenda Lee Eager
Omowale and Laura Elson
Damon Evans
M. Ena Ellis – Camille (Lorraine), Chris and Family
Alexis Estwick
Valerie Duncan Evans
Family Constellations, Maryland
Saundra K. Ford, Mark, Ramona and Joseph
Michael Forte'
Alethea Raynor Frazier
Verna Lucille Gardenhire
Rev. June Juliet Gatlin
Rev. Nirvana and Deborah Gayle
Donna Prescott and Steven Gaynor
Ava and Sherrell George
Dudley, Sr.(d) and Willie Mae George and Family
Eloise, Darren and Greg George
Homer George (d)
Rodney A. George, Patsy Brundidge George and Talib
Ron Gerard
Andrea Georgio
The Coreas and Gillems
Rodney Gittens, R.Sc.P.
Rev. Jeanette Glass (d)
Dr. Gochette and Carol
Cheryl Govia, R.Sc.P.
Tyler (Tutu) Grant
Miriam Green
Gayle and Wesley Greenwood
Guidance Church of Religious Science Family
Rev. Trish Hall
Grover Hampton
Rev. Daytra Hansel
Conchita and Robert Harris
Rev. Lelia Harris
Dr. Norma Harris
Dr. Maisha Hazzard
Eli Hawthorne
Howard Hrobak
R. Isoke Holmes

James Rogers
Rickey and Jamil Howell
Lloyd Dennis (d) and Monique Hunter
Yvonne M. Hyde, R.Sc.P.
Irene(d) and Troy, Vivian and Tony
Wilbert Jackson
The Jacques Family
Sonia Jackson
James Jeter (d) and Eunice Myles
Danny and Thomas Johnson
Dearie Johnson
Dr. JohnL. Johnson and Gladys Clark-Johnson
David Jones
Gary Jones and the Yuppets
Heather Jones, R.Sc.P.
Joyce Jones
Kevin Jones
McKinley Jordan
JulMar(d)
Rev. Linda Ketchum
Jeanne F. King, MA, MFT
Dafina Kuficha
Rev. Carrie Lauer
Amelia and Natalie Lawless
Rev. Juanita Lawrence
Richard Lawrence
Maura Laura LeBron
Tina Lifford
Lindy, Jada, Zoe, Angela, Keith, Max
Rev. Ruth Littlejohn
Amenta Jocelyn Lofton
Lorraine, Ramal, Golden, Loretta, Paula and Sierra
Eugene Lovick
Anita Luckey
Moqui Lund
Karen and Christian Drisdom Lusear
The Lyles
Gabriele Mack
Marilyn Mackel
Dawn and Isis Mancil
Eisha Mason, R.Sc.P.
Loretta Mason
Rev. Sherry and Rasheryl McCreary
Uncle and Auntie McElroy
Isaiah McGee
Rev. Kathy McNamara
Zenobia McNeil and Family
Sandra Middleton
Stacy V. Mills
Arny and Amy Mindell
The Mitchell Family - Ann, Paul(d), Bernice, Stevie
The Mitchell Family - Aunt Johnnie, Wesley, Chester
and Carolyn
Dr. Daniel L. Morgan (d)
The Moses'
Sameerah Muhammad
Arthur Murray (d)
Eunice Myles and James Jeter (d)
The NASDB Members and Associates
Deloris Nash
Darryl Newton (d) and Kay (d) and Conley (d)
Rev. Zuri Nia
Dr. Rev. Queen Adwoa Nyamekye
The entire O'Neal, Slater and Stovall Clans
The Pacific Bell and AT&T Group
Cousin Marjorie (d), Eugene, Zackary Parker Family
Johnny Parker, R.Sc.P.
Mshinda Parvenux, R.Sc.P.
Paul (d), Arlena (d), Carlaya and Paul Jr.
Llewellyn Peniston
Rev. Sheila Pierce
Pamela J. Pilate (d) and Family
Rev. Gregory Pitts and Family
The Harris and Pleasant Family
Process Oriented Psychology Organization
Edryce, Chris, Ellis and Ioie

Emerald Rainbow
Rev. Cheryl Rose
Anne Roise
The Rossi Family – Mrs. Rossi, Anita, Nolan(d),
Clinton, Pamela, Kimberly
The Rucker Family
St. Anthony nuns, staff, class and schoolmates
St. Leo nuns, priest, staff, class and schoolmates
Royetta, Aaron, Lorenzo and Aaron, Carla and Lauren
Monty Sanders, SLAP
Sanford and Family
Savannah Science of Mind Study Group
Savannah Friends
Ester Scott
Rev. Yusuf and Bishop Estella Shabazz and Family
Rev. Theresa Shields and Sandra Williams, Esq. and
Family
Max Schupbach, Ph.D.
David and Joshua Silverstein
Charles, Deloris, Fatima (d), Eloise, Evelyn, Nan,
Gordon, Rushkin, Kay, Mary Beth, Ruth, Leatrice,
Marilyn, Amie, Dory, Raoul, Bill Frey, Muriel,
Chemise Smith
Pastor Kenny Smith
The South African New Thought Groups
Rev. Lissa Sprinkles
Rev. Joan Stedman
Tommi Stephens and Lorraine
Steward
Daniel Sturdivant
Rev. Sylvia Sumter
The Swain Family
B.T. Taylor and Marlon
Rev. Antoinette J. Tibbs
Janie R. Tisdale
Rev. Carol Traylor (d) and Amber
Abeba and Lene Tsegaye
Edward Turley
UMUC
Nia Ujamaa and Family
Larry Vann
Janine Vaughn
Cape Verde Children
Gino Walker
Cousin Tom (d), Ann, Marguerite and Bernice and
The entire Waller Clan
Mark Warlick
Ronnie Washington
Spencer (d) and Edith Bell Watson (d)
Hon. Diane E. Watson
Leon Watson
Rabiya L. Watson
Rodney A. Watson (d)
Rylona A. Watson
Theodora L. Wesley Watson (d)
The Wilkins
William A. L. F. Watson I (d)
William A. L. F. Watson, II and Chetera Watson and
Allen, Cesiley, Ryan, Calysta, Niles, Alexys, Chetera and Iris
The Websters
Rev. Jim Webb
West Los Angeles Community College
Marilyn, Robert, Donna and Donnis (d) White Family
Wyllene L. Watson Wilfong
The Hon. Henry T. Wilfong, Jr.
The Wilfong Family: Henry T. (d) and Geraldine (d)
Wilfong, Sr.; Bernetta, Kevin and Daughters, Brian
and Justin; Barbara Jean and Family
Will
Rev. Carol (Winston) Williams
The Michael Williams Family
Betty Wilson, R.Sc.P.
Rev. Thomas Carl Wilson
Kermit Woodson
Rev. Brenda Woods
Dr. Jerry Wright

To all of my relations who are not mentioned in the Appreciation and Gratitude List - the list just kept getting longer and longer – you are in my heart. I prosper and thrive because of your presence –
I thank you.

To my sons, Rodney A. George and Damion A. Davis, thank you for coming through me to be your parent. You keep me conscious. I Love you.

A special thank you to my little ones who I cherish more than words can express: Rashid George, Janiya George, Josiah George, and Brooklynne R. Vaughn-Davis.

And, to my husband, Hank Wilfong, Jr., you kept the lights on.
I thank you and I love you.

To those who worked the practice, edited, were a sounding board, and gave advice and consultation, I thank you:

Rev. Trish Hall

R. Isoke Holmes

Yvonne M. Hyde, R.Sc.P.

Dr. JohnL. Johnson

Jeanne F. King, MA, MFT

Gabriele Mack

Stacy V. Mills

Dr. Rev. Queen Adwoa Nyamekye

Johnny Parker, R.Sc.P.

Angela Shaw, R.Sc.P.

Gino Walker

Rylona A. Watson

Rev. Thomas Carl Wilson

INTRODUCTION

Forgiveness is imperative. Forgiveness is the action that frees the soul of past transgressions. We are human and we will make missteps, blunders, horrendous actions and sometimes some actions are just wrong. It's a fact of life. And, we must be able to own up to our errors; learn from them and then move on. Holding onto guilt and grudges breed pain, resentment, fear and a whole lot of anxiety; and these unhealthy emotions build up toxicities in the mind, body and spirit. We have power, intellect and a heart. We can use them as we want to; however, forgiveness is imperative to be free.

This 40-Day *Intentional* Forgiveness Practice, with the emphasis on *Intentional*, is designed for you to be an active participant in the practice of forgiveness to keep you mentally clear, emotionally clean, and totally healthy.

> *"Not rendering evil for evil, or railing for railing; but instead of these render blessings; for to this end you have been called; that you may inherit a blessing.." Holy Bible. I Peter 3:9*

Our mandate is to live an abundant life of joy, love, peace, beauty, prosperity, and good will. We cannot fully live holding onto past behaviors and actions of ourselves and others. If we do not forgive, we hold in a space within ourselves something that cannot serve our greater good; and whatever it is, it takes up room – it is burdensome. When we forgive and give up what is held onto, an opening occurs for ourselves to reveal more of our greatness and good will, and to receive blessings for our lives.

At the time of our birth, we are given inalienable rights for our safekeeping and protection – such as the *Ten* Commandments: the thou shalls and shall nots. These are boundaries given to us as our birthright; and when they are violated, the violation makes clear what is and is not acceptable. We can feel the violation in our bones when a boundary has been infringed upon. And, when we don't own up to it or acknowledge the errors, we are allowing our boundaries to be disrespected and violated, again and again and again … we invalidate our importance; and, we allow someone else to set our boundaries. Therefore, it is absolutely necessary that we forgive to regain our self-respect, dignity, self-worth, true power and insight to define who we are … from this, we shall prosper.

> *"We are not our actions but we can become our actions; and if they are not becoming to us or healthy for us, we can make another decision."*
> *—W. L. Watson Wilfong*

We may ask ourselves, why am I not moving in the direction I want to go? Because there is an underlying influence that keeps us making decisions that are not for our highest good. When we *intentionally* look into the inner walls of our souls, we can have insights that give us clarity on what is holding us back. We can then make different decisions that direct and keep us on our path to our freedom; thus, we prosper.

We are perfect in Spirit. However, there are times when we have not lived up to our perfection. Be forgiving, and where apologies are needed, apologize. This is how we prosper. When we let go of violations, we allow ourselves to heal the wounds inflicted upon ourselves and others and we become whole again.

Within this workbook there is a Glossary to use as a reference point, an instruction to prepare yourself for the daily exercises; and, the daily exercises. Whether we know it or accept it or not, we are impacted by many variables in life which tailor our belief and behavior systems. I have prepared this workbook to take into account these variables. The exercises begin with you, then family, intimate and other relationships, local, federal and global institutions, wars, money, health, and ends with you.

This is your life so take responsibility for it. Be kindhearted to yourself as you do this 40-day *Intentional* Forgiveness Practice. State your *intention* as to why this forgiveness practice is important for you and what you *intend* to reconcile; and, what you will gain from the reconciliation. Be in principle: We are created to live in joy, happiness, love, wellness, and perfect health—to have a sound mind, to thrive and to prosper; and grace undergirds them all. Be truthful: If you judge yourself and someone else, look deeply into the judgment as to why you are holding onto the judgment. NO MORE VICTIM. Set your bar high! Make this practice important for you.

There may be intense resistance to do forgiveness work which gives you more reason to do it, because you are not free. Mark your calendar for the 40-day commitment and take it one day at a time. You have invisible and visible Divine support systems. Call upon them as you need your support. Don't be bashful, don't be shy, and don't let ego get in the way. Ask for support.

Know that as you forgive, grace has a place to guide and direct you onto a path of total fulfillment. How do you forgive, you ask? You forgive, *tenderly.*

"Be transformed by the renewing of your mind." Holy Bible, Romans (12:2)

This 40-Day *Intentional* Forgiveness Practice may not be reproduced in any manner without prior consent from the Author. Thank you. W. L. Watson Wilfong, R.Sc.P. (Prepared June 2010.)

QUOTES

"Wyllene Watson has much to teach us about Forgiveness. Her insightful work is a core element of what our world needs in order to eventually resolve long-standing conflicts." —Arnold Mindell, author of *The Deep Democracy of Open Forums*

This process was all about "having the courage to dialogue with yourself about yourself to reveal your higher self." —Rev. Dr. Queen Adwoa Nyamekye

"There is an African (Yoruba) proverb that says, 'The person who forgives achieves victory.' Forgiveness is only a step on the pathway to atonement, which takes place in a process called time. The most important act of forgiveness that one can offer is how to forgive one's self for remaining silent in the face of poverty and injustice throughout the world." —JohnL. Johnson, EdM, Adjunct Professor, University Mary Washington, Diplomate of Process Oriented Psychology

"Wyllene Watson-Wilfong brings depth and compassion to the subject of forgiveness. Her wisdom guides the reader through personal evolution to a new way of being present in the world. Wyllene and her work are truly making the world a better place by fostering release of the tensions of unhealed wounds and movement toward health on all levels of mind, body, and spirit." —Rev. Trish Hall, Senior Minister, Celebration Center of Spiritual Living, Falls Church, Virginia

"Forgiveness for others is an acknowledgement, by you, that you have allowed someone to commit a transgression upon your person. But the most important act of forgiveness is to forgive yourself for your participation in the transgression." —Jeanne F. King, MA, MFT

"The act and the reaction are separate. The act is one thing; the reaction is another." —W. L. Watson Wilfong, R.Sc.P.

"In life there are no friends or enemies, only teachers." —Kitty Nellums

QUOTES ON FORGIVENESS

"Not even who the Son of God (that's you) made in insanity could be without a hidden spark of beauty that gentleness could release. All this beauty will rise to your sight as you look upon the world with forgiving eyes. For forgiveness literally transforms vision, and lets you see the real world reaching quietly and gently across chaos, removing all illusions that had twisted your perception and fixed it on the past. The smallest leaf becomes a thing of wonder and a blade of grass a sign of God's perfection. From the forgiven world, the Son of God is lifted easily into his home. And there he knows that he has always rested in peace." A Course in Miracles, Vol. 1.

"The mind which condemns, understands not the truth of being, and the heart which would shut the door of its bosom to one who is mistaken, strangles its own life, closing its eyes to a greater vision. The biggest life is one which includes the most. To him who loves much, much is forgiven." —Words that Heal Today. Ernest Holmes.

GLOSSARY

40: The number 40 represents creation, rebirth; time of maturation; spiritual defeat of physical and emotional habits; period of revival, renewal, probation. It leads to enlarged territories – dominion; points to the action of grace.

ABUSE: The physical, psychological, or sexual maltreatment of a person or animal. Illegal, improper or harmful use and practice of something and someone; insulting or offensive language; cruel treatment to a person or animal.

ACTION: Movement, deed, exploit, achievement, feat, engagement, encounter, clash, combat, prosecution, to punish, to harm, to debase, to victimize, to love, to heal, to hold harmless, to criticize, to hurt, to cause pain, to ignore, to acknowledge, to gossip, to enjoy, to have pleasure, and so on.

ALLEGIANCE: Duty, adherence, loyalty.

ANIMOSITY: Hatred, Ill will, bitterness, acrimony, rancor, dislike, antagonism.

ASHE': Strong agreement; affirmation of content.

ATONEMENT: Christianity. The reconciliation of God and humans brought about by the redemptive life and death of Jesus the Christ; Compensation for a wrong; admission of wrongdoing; remorse.

BEHAVIOR SYSTEMS: The way a person, organism, or group responds to a specific set of conditions.

BETRAYAL: Violation of trust and confidence, promise; disloyal.

BELIEF SYSTEMS: A collection of beliefs prevalent in a person, community and society that form a unified system.

BOUNDARY: A sacred encasement which holds the principles, laws, morals, and values of a person; A person's private life. The ethical standard of a person: trust, power, respect and honor, accountability, responsibility; personal space, physicality and property; The Ten commandments; personal laws and property lines which involved parties must have an agreement to trespass and or compromise; violation of boundaries such as probing into another's life, misuse of property and person, going into a person's personal belongings without permission.

BOUNTIFUL: Plenitude, to be eclectic, cornucopia of life, to engage in many ventures.

COMPROMISE: To undermine, devalue somebody or something; to agree to accept less than what was wanted; to expose somebody or something to danger or disgrace; willingness to lower standards; to tolerate a substandard lifestyle; to knowingly forfeit power to someone or something.

DEMEANED: To degrade, debase, humiliate, put down, and gossip, demoralize.

DISHONOR: Loss of respect; good reputation; cause of shame.

DIVINE SUPPORT SYSTEM: Spirit; God; Creator; Supernatural – Invisible Presence; An underlying creative and a sustaining Force in the Universe.

ERROR: The fact of acting wrongly or misguidedly; acting out from incorrect beliefs and opinions; something un*intentionally* done wrong, result of poor judgment or lack of care; false assumptions; of being inappropriate or unacceptable.

FAHTHER: Spelled *intentionally* fAHther to emphasize the "*ah*" sound to raise the vibration of love.

FALSE POWER: Manipulative, coercion, making decisions from resentment, shame, fear, blame, guilt, revenge, pain, heartbreak, rage, hostility, and a weakened state of confidence and self-esteem.

FEAR: An emotion which takes over true power, clarity of thought, and natural senses; causes paranoia, pain, illness and false beliefs.

FORGIVENESS: Releasing the behavior and action of another and/or self from hostage and bondage; allowing oneself and/or another to become free.

GOD'S REALM: True power; pure love to be carried and supported by life without effort.

GRACE: Accepting and allowing yourself to be carried and supported by life without effort.

GRATITUDE: Appreciation for something and someone, recognizing and acknowledging the value of something and someone, grateful. (No matter how difficult the experience was/is give thanks for it).

GRIEF: Feeling and expression of intense deep and profound sorrow, pain, and great sadness as a result of death, an event or situation; loss of a loved one; loss of a position; loss of an identity; loss of purpose.

HUMOR: Laughter; a way to release blockages; change the concepts and perceptions of an experience; bring lightness and light to an experience; to gain a healthy resolve.

INHERENT: Within the whole nature of a being. A natural makeup of life.

INTENTIONAL: Deliberate, conscious involvement, activation of intention.

INTRAPERSONAL REFLECTIONS: Relating to the internal aspects of a person, especially emotions; careful thought, the process of reconsidering previous actions, events or decisions; a cause of blame or credit to somebody and or something.

JEALOUSY: Feeling bitter because of another's possessions, advantages, envious, possessive, obsessive and territorial, invidious, mistrustful, resentful.

JOURNAL: A free style form of writing to document and to release thoughts, feelings, words, actions, and deeds of anyone; a form of catharsis.

JUDGEMENT: A criticism against a character, behavior, action, thought process, past/ current experience of an individual or one self.

KINDHEARTED: Caring, compassionate, gentle, merciful.

LOVE: To be devoted to, to care for, to be fond of, to be in adoration of, and to hold in high regard.

LOYALTY: An allegiance, commitment, faithfulness, constancy, reliability, fidelity.

MISSTEP: An error in conduct. And, as in MISTAKE, an experience to learn from and to be empowered by.

MISTAKE: A mistake is a decision made from ignorance. An incorrect, unwise or unfortunate act, choice, or decision; lack of judgment or information; an experience to learn from and to be empowered by.

OPPRESSION: To impede; to cause an impediment for growth, expansion, self expression; source of worry, stress, or trouble to somebody; domination over thoughts, feelings, expressions of freedom; something that hinders progress; an interference; an interruption to movement and development.

PLEASURES: Expressions of creativity; gratification of joy, recreation, relaxation, especially sexual enjoyment; happiness; delight to the senses, spiritual elevation

POWER SCALE: A gauge to determine one's level of power in certain situations, thoughts, experiences, memories, principles: (Power Scale from 1 being weakest to 10 being strongest.)

Power scale 1|_2|_3|_4|_5|_6|_7|_8|_9|_10|_

PRAYER: The evocation of a desire to come into form- help, wellness, change; a devotion of spoken words to God, deity, saint;

PRINCIPLES: An important underlying law that is inherent and innate of oneself. The primary gauge for respect/disrespect, honor/dishonor. The standard for self-identification/ self-knowing.

PROTECTION: To safeguard someone; to keep from being physically, mentally, emotionally, harmed or damaged.

R.Sc.P.: Religious Science Practitioner licensed as a Spiritual Counselor by The Center For Spiritual Living headquartered in Colorado (formerly, United Church of Religious Science).

REALM: Area or domain; a scope of something; a defined area of interest.

RECONCILIATION: The ending of conflict or renewing of a relationship between disputing people, groups and most importantly the end of a personal internal conflict.

RETROSPECT: Thinking about or reviewing the past, especially from a new perspective or with new information.

SACRED: To cherish and regard with respect, honor, adoration, devotion, and love.

SEAT OF THE SOUL: Sitting in a panoramic position to view every aspect of the soul.

SECRET LOVER: An authentic expression kept under guard.

SOCIAL INSTITUTIONS: Social institutions are patterns of beliefs and behaviors centered on basic social needs. Essentially different elements of society. Examples include, schools, workplace, religious institutions, family, polity, financial institutions, and socio-economic structures .

SOUL: Essence, heart, character, core, inner self.

SPIRIT: Force and source, moral fiber, mettle, resolve.

SPIRITUAL COUNSELOR: Someone who applies spiritual principles in assisting a person to reveal their greater self; relating to the soul or spirit; seeing the sacredness, perfection, and love within a person beyond any actions to the contrary; an intercessory on someone's behalf.

SPIRITUAL OBSERVER: Beholding all activities and assessing them without judgment. Detached from actions, behaviors, emotions, past and present experiences, circumstances, situations, insinuations, and suggestions.

SPIRITUAL PRACTICE: A daily spiritual ritual; a time of introspection, contemplation, self-assessment, meditation; a quiet time to set the tone for the day and reviewing participation in the day; journaling; honoring your presence within your soul; acknowledging your spiritual source of power, love, wisdom, intelligence; giving thanksgiving for everyone and everything; giving thanksgiving to God/Creator/Supreme Being/Allah/Jehovah/Elohim/Jesus the Christ/the Universe/the source of your love and life. Daily readings of a sacred text; listening and singing soul stirring music; dancing; feeding your soul, mind and body in a reverential manner.

SPIRITUAL PRINCIPLES: Perfection, unlimited abundance; unconditional love; wholeness; unlimited universal intelligence; Perfection in spirit, health, mind, body and soul; an important underlying law and assumption required in a system of thought; a basic way in which something works; God; a primary source of someone.

STREET SENSE: An unsupervised unstructured adaptation for survival; being self taught of how to toughen survival muscles and skills; strengthening the inner constitution; and, being street smart.

STREET CULTURE: Designed ways of expression which are unlike mainstream society; example: gang colors, gang hand signs, gang clothing, tagging, etc.

SUGGESTIONS: Language, customs, roles, rules, moral values, guidelines; race thoughts that are part of cultures, factual scientific research, governments, and intimations; and historical data that influence choices and decisions.

SYSTEMIC: Relating to the generational system; the familial system; the ancestral system, a predecessor of somebody and something.

TEN COMMANDMENTS/BIBLICAL RULES: The summary of human obligations to self, each other, and God.

TENDERLY: Showing care, gentleness and feeling; sensitive caring toward another and yourself; a tender disposition and reconciliation.

TRANCE: Daze, stupor, spell, sleep, reverie.

TRUE POWER: No pretension of being. Power used with firm, faithful confidence; and, with clarity, grace, and ease, honesty, forthrightness, authenticity and discernment.

VICTIM: Hurt, deprived freedom, adversely affected by action or circumstance; tricked or exploited; being misused; feeling of powerlessness; feeling emotionally, mentally, physically, socially, culturally, politically, and/or financially strapped, wronged.

VIOLATION: Crossing the personal boundaries of another without permission. An infringement of personal space and property. Breaking and or disrespecting a law; the act of violating.

PREPARATION FOR THE 40-DAY
INTENTIONAL FORGIVENESS PRACTICE

Set aside time each day to work this practice. This is for your healing, evolvement, and growth. This is your opportunity to shed unwanted ways, thoughts, actions, and behaviors that have had you encumbered, enslaved, and functioning in a trance state.

Create your space as a sacred chamber for this practice. Have a lighted candle for your ever-vigilant light that you are; a bowl of water* to move blocked, old, and stagnant energy and to keep energy flowing; if desired, have very soft background music**; a Journal and pen/pencil to write your thoughts of what may come to mind and to release your feelings during the practice; and, a mirror to see yourself as the one who is responsible for creating your life the way you want it to be.

Sit in silence for ten to fifteen minutes to prepare for the work. Allow yourself to know as you start each practice that you are safe and secure and that nothing can harm you. You are held in the arms of Spirit – You are protected. Call upon an ancestor(s)/angel(s) to be with you during these 40-days. State your intention - your reason(s) why. (How would you like to feel; What would you like to have resolved? Who/what would you like to have a better relationship with, etc.) Bless this time you will spend with yourself and then begin the practice. Accept that as you release through forgiveness, you are giving yourself and others a wonderful gift ... so be kindhearted to yourself and about others. Note: We hold onto the past when we are afraid to let ourselves experience the richness and wealth of who we truly are. Forgiveness is about you!!! And, remember to forgive, tenderly.

At the end of each practice, pray a prayer of thanksgiving and end, while looking into the mirror, with the words: "I have *intentionally* forgiven myself, and my boundaries are _____. Peace . . . peace . . . peace."

Above all else, remember to have humor.

*Water: After each exercise dispose of it outside.

**See Suggested Music

SUGGESTED MUSIC

"A Change is Gonna Come" performed by Rebecca Ferguson X Factor Audition – originally performed by Sam Cooke

"Alone in His Presence" album performed by CeCe Winans

"Besame Mucho" performed by Cesaria Evora

"Butterflies" and "Man in the Mirror" performed by Michael Jackson

"Changed" performed by Tramaine Hawkins

"Empire State of Mind" performed by Alicia Keys and Jay-Z

"Feeling Good" performed by Nina Simone

"God's Gift to the World" and "Pieces of a Heart" performed by Carl Anderson

"Tears in Heaven" performed by Gregorian

"Gregorian Chant" Kyrie Christe Eleison – Lord Have Mercy!

"Higher Ground" performed by Stevie Wonder

"Hold On", "I Believe", and "Optimistic" performed by Sounds of Blackness

"Hush" performed by Gino Walker

"I'm Changed" performed by the Agape International Choir, featuring Beverly Freeman

"I'm Living Proof" performed by Mary J. Blige

"I Rest In Thee" performed by Rickie Byars Beckwith and Carl Anderson

"I Surrender All" performed by Coalo Zamorano and Michael W. Smith

"I Thank You" performed by Rickie Byars Beckwith

"I Want to Thank You" performed by Alicia Myers

"Let Go" performed by Dewayne Woods

"Little Fly" performed by Esperanza Spalding

"Music in the Age of Pyramids" performed by Rafael Perez Arroyo

"Open My Heart" performed by Yolanda Adams

"Power of Soul" and "State of Mind" performed by Marcus Miller

"The Romantic Warrior" Return to Forever IV World Tour 2011 performances by: Chick Corea: keys; Stanley Clarke: bass; Lenny White: drums; Jean-Luc Ponty: violin; Frank Gambale: guitar

"Sing Through My Heart" performed by Miriam Green accompanied by the Agape International Choir

"Tears Dry on Their Own" performed by Amy Winehouse

"What's Going On?" performed by Marvin Gaye

"Wisdom" performed by Gregory Porter

"Your Best is Yet to Come" Performed by Niki Haris and New Thought at Agape International Spiritual Center

DAY ONE

Remember my preparation time and state my intention.

As I sit in the seat of my soul, I spiritually observe the temperament of my emotions that come up around forgiveness. I observe the feelings of the known and am prepared to be made aware of the unknown past experiences that I am to forgive and release. I set my intention to forgive and release.

What emotions are being felt? Fear, tension, anger, shame, embarrassment, sadness, quilt, hurt, acceptance, betrayal, strength, courage, rage, time for closure, resolve, and etc.

Be honest and forthright with myself. Journal:

Which boundaries were dishonored, disrespected, violated, and compromised?

How have my emotions and behavior impacted my true power? Assess where my true power is on a scale of 1 to 10.

Power scale 1|_2|_3|_4|_5|_6|_7|_8|_9|_10|_

Journal:

I *intentionally* forgive myself for holding onto past experiences known and unknown that I have been afraid to confront and/or let go of.

What am I feeling right now?

Journal:

Establish boundaries.

I clarified and established my boundaries, which are _____ .

I appreciate myself today because _____ .

Pray a prayer of thanksgiving and end, while looking into the mirror, with the words: "I have *intentionally* forgiven myself, and my boundaries are _____ _____ .

Peace ... peace ... peace."

Reassess my true power.

Power scale 1|_2|_3|_4|_5|_6|_7|_8|_9|_10|_

There may be an overflow of feelings and thoughts; continue to journal when necessary.

DAY TWO

Remember my preparation time and state my intention.

As I sit in the seat of my soul, I spiritually observe and scan over my life to see what I have accomplished. I ask myself, am I accomplished in my passion? Did I compromise my passion for survival? Where have I shortchanged myself? Have I ever lived out of desperation?

Be honest and forthright with myself. Journal:

Which boundaries were dishonored, disrespected, violated, and compromised?

How have my emotions and behavior impacted my true power? Assess where my true power is on a scale of 1 to 10.

Power scale 1|_2|_3|_4|_5|_6|_7|_8|_9|_10|_

Journal:

I *intentionally* forgive myself for compromising my passion. I *intentionally* forgive myself for not trusting my decision to live a fully vibrant and passionate life.

Journal:

What am I feeling right now?

Journal:

Establish boundaries.

I clarified and established my boundaries, which are _____.

I appreciate myself today because _____.

Pray a prayer of thanksgiving and end, while looking into the mirror, with the words: "I have *intentionally* forgiven myself, and my boundaries are _____
_____.

Peace ... peace ... peace."

Reassess my true power.

Power scale 1|_2|_3|_4|_5|_6|_7|_8|_9|_10|_

There may be an overflow of feelings and thoughts; continue to journal when necessary.

DAY THREE

Remember my preparation time and state my intention.

As I sit in the seat of my soul, I spiritually observe where I am in my life and the influences in my life, particularly my mother. How did my mother influence any of my decisions of where I am today? Am I grateful to and for her? Did I dismiss anything she told me? Are there any grudges and anger toward my mother? Do I appreciate my mother?

Be honest and forthright with myself. Journal:

Which boundaries were dishonored, disrespected, violated, and compromised?

How have my emotions and behavior impacted my true power? Where is my true power on a scale of 1 to 10?

Power scale 1|_2|_3|_4|_5|_6|_7|_8|_9|_10|_

Journal:

As I contemplate my relationship with my mother, I *intentionally* forgive _____.

What am I feeling right now?

Journal:

Establish boundaries.

I clarified and established my boundaries, which are _____,

Journal:

I appreciate myself today because _____,

Pray a prayer of thanksgiving and end, while looking into the mirror, with the words: "I have *intentionally* forgiven myself, and my boundaries are _____

_____,

Peace ... peace ... peace."

Reassess my true power.

Power scale 1|_2|_3|_4|_5|_6|_7|_8|_9|_10|_

There may be an overflow of feelings and thoughts; continue to journal when necessary.

DAY FOUR

Remember my preparation time and state my intention.

As I sit in the seat of my soul, I spiritually observe my feelings as I recall what I may have expected of my mother. What did I expect of my mother? Were there disappointments? Have I carried any of those disappointments into my character and my values? How did those disappointments, if any, impact my choices as an adult? Was I protected and or betrayed by my mother?

Be honest and forthright with myself. Journal:

Which boundaries were dishonored, disrespected, violated, and compromised?

How have my emotions and behavior impacted my true power? Where is my true power on a scale of 1 to 10?

Power scale 1|_2|_3|_4|_5|_6|_7|_8|_9|_10|_

Journal:

Who shall be forgiven? I *intentionally* forgive _____.

Journal:

What am I feeling right now?

Journal:

Establish boundaries.

I clarified and established my boundaries, which are _____.

I appreciate myself today because _____.

Pray a prayer of thanksgiving and end, while looking into the mirror, with the words: "I have *intentionally* forgiven myself, and my boundaries are _____

_____.

Peace ... peace ... peace."

Reassess my true power.

Power scale 1|_2|_3|_4|_5|_6|_7|_8|_9|_10|_

There may be an overflow of feelings and thoughts; continue to journal when necessary.

DAY FIVE

Remember my preparation time and state my intention.

As I sit in the seat of my soul, I spiritually observe my feelings as I reflect about my mother. Are there any unconscious or conscious punitive behaviors and guilt feelings about my thoughts and feelings toward my mother? Did/do I love and care about my mother? What are my true feelings about my mother? I could not have been here without my mother. Is there something to say or write to my mother?

Be honest and forthright with myself. Journal:

Which boundaries were dishonored, disrespected, violated, and compromised?

How have my emotions and behavior impacted my true power? Where is my true power on a scale of 1 to 10?

Power scale 1|_2|_3|_4|_5|_6|_7|_8|_9|_10|_

Journal:

Who shall be forgiven? I *intentionally* forgive _____,

Journal:

What am I feeling right now?

Journal:

Establish boundaries.

I clarified and established my boundaries, which are _____,

I appreciate myself today because _____,

Pray a prayer of thanksgiving and end, while looking into the mirror, with the words: "I have *intentionally* forgiven myself, and my boundaries are _____

_____

Peace ... peace ... peace."

Power scale 1|_2|_3|_4|_5|_6|_7|_8|_9|_10|_

There may be an overflow of feelings and thoughts; continue to journal when necessary.

DAY SIX

Remember my preparation time and state my intention.

As I sit in the seat of my soul, I contemplate my overall feelings about my mother, and I spiritually observe to see where I am emotionally and how I am feeling about my mother and myself. What type of person was/is she and am I now, as a result of the past days of reflection and forgiveness? Any revelations, "ahas"? Any changes in my feelings about my mother and myself?

Be honest and forthright with myself. Journal:

Which boundaries were dishonored, disrespected, violated, and compromised?

How have my emotions and behavior impacted my true power? Where is my true power on a scale of 1 to 10?

Power scale 1|_2|_3|_4|_5|_6|_7|_8|_9|_10|_

Journal:

Who shall be forgiven as I contemplate my relationship with my mother?
I *intentionally* forgive _____.

Journal:

What am I feeling right now?

Journal:

Establish boundaries.

I clarified and established my boundaries, which are _____,

I appreciate myself today because, _____,

Pray a prayer of thanksgiving and end, while looking into the mirror, with the words: "I have *intentionally* forgiven myself, and my boundaries are _____
_____.

Peace ... peace ... peace."

Reassess my true power.

Power scale 1|_2|_3|_4|_5|_6|_7|_8|_9|_10|_

There may be an overflow of feelings and thoughts; continue to journal when necessary.

DAY SEVEN

Remember my preparation time and state my intention.

As I sit in the seat of my soul, I think about my maternal grandparents. As I spiritually observe, what do I feel about them? What kind of relationship do I have or did I have with them—my grandmother and grandfather? What did/do I cherish about knowing them? Did I know them as well as I could have? Is there a feeling of loss and dissatisfaction—or fullness and satisfaction about the relationships? How have they influenced my life?

Be honest and forthright with myself. Journal:

Which boundaries were dishonored, disrespected, violated, and compromised?

How have my emotions and behavior impacted my true power? Where is my true power on a scale of 1 to 10?

Power scale 1|_2|_3|_4|_5|_6|_7|_8|_9|_10|_

Journal:

Who shall be forgiven? I *intentionally* forgive _____.

Journal:

What am I feeling right now?

Journal:

Establish boundaries.

I clarified and established my boundaries, which are _____.

I appreciate myself today because _____.

Pray a prayer of thanksgiving and end, while looking into the mirror, with the words: "I have *intentionally* forgiven myself, and my boundaries are _____

_____.

Peace ... peace ... peace."

Reassess my true power.

Power scale 1|_2|_3|_4|_5|_6|_7|_8|_9|_10|_

There may be an overflow of feelings and thoughts; continue to journal when necessary.

DAY EIGHT

Remember my preparation time and state my intention.

We take on systemic behaviors and actions of our ancestors because of our allegiance, loyalty, acceptance, and lack of self-knowing, or to keep the perpetuation of a story whether it serves us or not.

As I sit in the seat of my soul, I spiritually observe as I look upon my behaviors, habits, and actions, and I ask to bring forth that within me that is a replication of my maternal ancestors. Does it serve me? Am I fruitful for this behavior? Am I oppressing myself because of this behavior? What have I gained from it, and what do I anticipate to gain from it?

Be honest and forthright with myself. Journal:

Which boundaries were dishonored, disrespected, violated, and compromised?

How have my emotions and behavior impacted my true power? Where is my true power on a scale of 1 to 10?

Power scale 1|_2|_3|_4|_5|_6|_7|_8|_9|_10|_

Journal:

Who shall be forgiven? I *intentionally* forgive _____.

Journal:

What am I feeling right now?

Journal:

Establish boundaries.

I clarified and established my boundaries, which are _____.

I appreciate myself today because _____.

Pray a prayer of thanksgiving and end, while looking into the mirror, with the words: "I have *intentionally* forgiven myself, and my boundaries are _____
_____.

Peace ... peace ... peace."

Reassess my true power.

Power scale 1|_2|_3|_4|_5|_6|_7|_8|_9|_10|_

There may be an overflow of feelings and thoughts; continue to journal when necessary.

DAY NINE

Remember my preparation time and state my intention.

As I sit in the seat of my soul, I spiritually observe my feelings as I think about my relationship with my father. How did my father influence any of my decisions of where I am today? Am I grateful to and for him? Did I dismiss anything he told me? Are there any grudges and anger toward my father? Do I appreciate my father?

Be honest and forthright with myself. Journal:

Which boundaries were dishonored, disrespected, violated, and compromised?

How have my emotions and behavior impacted my true power? Where is my true power on a scale of 1 to 10?

Power scale 1|_2|_3|_4|_5|_6|_7|_8|_9|_10|_

Journal:

Who shall be forgiven? I *intentionally* forgive _____,

Journal:

What am I feeling right now?

Journal:

Establish boundaries.

I clarified and established my boundaries, which are _____,

I appreciate myself today because _____,

Pray a prayer of thanksgiving and end, while looking into the mirror, with the words: "I have *intentionally* forgiven myself, and my boundaries are _____

_____

Peace ... peace ... peace."

Reassess my true power.

Power scale 1|_2|_3|_4|_5|_6|_7|_8|_9|_10|_

There may be an overflow of feelings and thoughts; continue to journal when necessary.

DAY TEN

Remember my preparation time and state my intention.

As I sit in the seat of my soul, I spiritually observe my feelings as I recall what I may have expected of my father. What did I expect of my father? Were there disappointments? Have I carried any of those disappointments into my character and my values? How do those disappointments, if any, impact my choices as an adult? Was I protected and or betrayed by my father?

Be honest and forthright with myself. Journal:

Which boundaries were dishonored, disrespected, violated, and compromised?

How have my emotions and behavior impacted my true power? Where is my true power on a scale of 1 to 10?

$$\text{Power scale } 1|\_2|\_3|\_4|\_5|\_6|\_7|\_8|\_9|\_10|\_$$

Journal:

Who shall be forgiven? I *intentionally* forgive _____.

Journal:

What am I feeling right now?

Journal:

Establish boundaries.

I clarified and established my boundaries, which are _____.

I appreciate myself today because _____.

Pray a prayer of thanksgiving and end, while looking into the mirror, with the words: "I have *intentionally* forgiven myself, and my boundaries are _____

_____.

Peace ... peace ... peace."

Reassess my true power.

$$\text{Power scale } 1|\_2|\_3|\_4|\_5|\_6|\_7|\_8|\_9|\_10|\_$$

There may be an overflow of feelings and thoughts; continue to journal when necessary.

DAY ELEVEN

Remember my preparation time and state my intention.

As I sit in the seat of my soul, I spiritually observe my feelings as I reflect about my father. Are there any unconscious or conscious punitive behaviors and guilt feelings about my thoughts and feelings toward my father? Did/do I love and care about my father? What are my true feelings about my father? I could not have been here without my father. Is there something to say or write to my father?

Be honest and forthright with myself. Journal:

Which boundaries were dishonored, disrespected, violated, and compromised?

How have my emotions and behavior impacted my true power? Where is my true power on a scale of 1 to 10?

Power scale 1|_2|_3|_4|_5|_6|_7|_8|_9|_10|_

Journal:

Who shall be forgiven? I *intentionally* forgive _____,

Journal:

What am I feeling right now?

Journal:

Establish boundaries.

I clarified and established my boundaries, which are _____,

I appreciate myself today because _____,

Pray a prayer of thanksgiving and end, while looking into the mirror, with the words: "I have *intentionally* forgiven myself, and my boundaries are _____

_____,

Peace ... peace ... peace."

Reassess my true power.

Power scale 1|_2|_3|_4|_5|_6|_7|_8|_9|_10|_

There may be an overflow of feelings and thoughts; continue to journal when necessary.

DAY TWELVE

Remember my preparation time and state my intention.

As I sit in the seat of my soul, I contemplate my overall feelings about my father, and I spiritually observe to see where I am emotionally and how I am feeling about my father and myself. What type of person was/is he and am I now, as a result of the past days of reflection and forgiveness? Any revelations, ahas? Any changes in my feelings about my father and myself?

Be honest and forthright with myself. Journal:

Which boundaries were dishonored, disrespected, violated, and compromised?

How have my emotions and behavior impacted my true power? Where is my true power on a scale of 1 to 10?

Power scale 1|_2|_3|_4|_5|_6|_7|_8|_9|_10|_

Journal:

Who shall be forgiven as I contemplate my relationship with my father?
I *intentionally* forgive _____,

Journal:

What am I feeling right now?

Journal:

Establish boundaries.

I clarified and established my boundaries, which are _____,

I appreciate myself today because _____,

Pray a prayer of thanksgiving and end, while looking into the mirror, with the words: "I have *intentionally* forgiven myself, and my boundaries are _____ _____,

Peace ... peace ... peace."

Reassess my true power.

Power scale 1|_2|_3|_4|_5|_6|_7|_8|_9|_10|_

There may be an overflow of feelings and thoughts; continue to journal when necessary.

12

DAY THIRTEEN

Remember my preparation time and state my intention.

As I sit in the seat of my soul, I think about my paternal grandparents. As I spiritually observe my emotions, what do I feel about them? What kind of relationship do I have or did I have with them—my grandmother and my grandfather? What did/do I cherish about knowing them? Did I know them as well as I could have? Is there a feeling of loss and dissatisfaction—or fullness and satisfaction about the relationships? How has their presence or absence influenced my life?

Be honest and forthright with myself. Journal:

Which boundaries were dishonored, disrespected, violated, and compromised?

How have my emotions and behavior impacted my true power? Where is my true power on a scale of 1 to 10?

Power scale 1|_2|_3|_4|_5|_6|_7|_8|_9|_10|_

Journal:

Who shall be forgiven? I *intentionally* forgive _____,

Journal:

What am I feeling right now?

Journal:

Establish boundaries.

I clarified and established my boundaries, which are _____,

I appreciate myself today because _____,

Pray a prayer of thanksgiving and end, while looking into the mirror, with the words: "I have *intentionally* forgiven myself, and my boundaries are _____

_____,

Peace ... peace ... peace."

Reassess my true power.

Power scale 1|_2|_3|_4|_5|_6|_7|_8|_9|_10|_

There may be an overflow of feelings and thoughts; continue to journal when necessary.

DAY FOURTEEN

Remember my preparation time and state my intention.

We take on systemic behaviors and actions of our ancestors because of our allegiance, loyalty, acceptance, and lack of self-knowing, or to keep the perpetuation of a story alive whether it serves us or not.

As I sit in the seat of my soul, I spiritually observe as I look upon my behaviors, habits, and actions, and I ask to bring forth that within me that is a replication of my paternal ancestors. What have I perpetuated? Does it serve me? Am I fruitful for this behavior? Am I oppressing myself and others because of this behavior? What have I gained from it? What do I anticipate to gain from it?

Be honest and forthright with myself. Journal:

Which boundaries were dishonored, disrespected, violated, and compromised?

How have my emotions and behavior impacted my true power? Where is my true power on a scale of 1 to 10?

Power scale 1|_2|_3|_4|_5|_6|_7|_8|_9|_10|_

Journal:

Who shall be forgiven? I *intentionally* forgive _____.

Journal:

What am I feeling right now?

Establish boundaries.

I clarified and established my boundaries, which are _____.

I appreciate myself today because _____.

Pray a prayer of thanksgiving and end, while looking into the mirror, with the words: "I have *intentionally* forgiven myself, and my boundaries are _____
_____.

Peace … peace … peace."

Reassess my true power.

Power scale 1|_2|_3|_4|_5|_6|_7|_8|_9|_10|_

There may be an overflow of feelings and thoughts; continue to journal when necessary.

DAY FIFTEEN

Remember my preparation time and state my intention.

We take on systemic behaviors, actions, and habits of our relatives because of our allegiance, loyalty, protection, acceptance, lack of self-knowing, or to keep the perpetuation of a story alive whether it serves us or not.

As I sit in the seat of my soul, I spiritually observe as I look upon my behaviors, habits, and actions, and I ask to bring forth the relationships with my maternal aunts, uncles, and cousins that may have halted my successes in life. What stories do I have of my maternal aunts, uncles, and cousins? What have I perpetuated? What are my habits, behaviors, and actions that reflect the relationship with my maternal aunts, uncles, and cousins? Do they serve me? Am I fruitful for these habits, behaviors, and actions? Am I oppressing myself and others because of these habits, behaviors, and actions? What have I gained from them? What do I anticipate to gain from them?

Be honest and forthright with myself. Journal:

Which boundaries were dishonored, disrespected, violated, and compromised?

How have my emotions and behavior impacted my true power? Where is my true power on a scale of 1 to 10?

Power scale 1|_2|_3|_4|_5|_6|_7|_8|_9|_10|_

Journal:

Who shall be forgiven? I *intentionally* forgive _____.

Journal:

What am I feeling right now?

Establish boundaries.

I clarified and established my boundaries, which are _____,

I appreciate myself today because _____,

Pray a prayer of thanksgiving and end, while looking into the mirror, with the words: "I have *intentionally* forgiven myself, and my boundaries are _____

_____

Peace ... peace ... peace."

Reassess my true power.

Power scale 1|_2|_3|_4|_5|_6|_7|_8|_9|_10|_

There may be an overflow of feelings and thoughts; continue to journal when necessary.

DAY SIXTEEN

Remember my preparation time and state my intention.

We take on systemic behaviors, actions, and habits of our relatives because of our allegiance, loyalty, protection, acceptance, lack of self-knowing, or to keep the perpetuation of a story alive whether it serves us or not.

As I sit in the seat of my soul, I spiritually observe as I look upon my behaviors, habits, and actions, and I ask to bring forth the relationships with my paternal aunts, uncles, and cousins that may have halted my successes in life. Do I perpetuate stories of my paternal aunts, uncles, and cousins? Are they healthy stories? What are my habits, behaviors, and actions that reflect the relationship with my paternal aunts, uncles, and cousins? Do they serve me? Am I fruitful for these habits, behaviors, and actions? Am I oppressing myself and others because of these habits, behaviors, and actions? What have I gained from them? What do I anticipate to gain from them?

Be honest and forthright with myself. Journal:

Which boundaries were dishonored, disrespected, violated, and compromised?

How have my emotions and behavior impacted my true power? Where is my true power on a scale of 1 to 10?

Power scale 1|_2|_3|_4|_5|_6|_7|_8|_9|_10|_

Journal:

Who shall be forgiven? I *intentionally* forgive _____.

Journal:

What am I feeling right now?

Establish boundaries.

I clarified and established my boundaries, which are _____.

I appreciate myself today because _____.

Pray a prayer of thanksgiving and end, while looking into the mirror, with the words: "I have *intentionally* forgiven myself, and my boundaries are _____ _____

Peace ... peace ... peace."

Reassess my true power.

Power scale 1|_2|_3|_4|_5|_6|_7|_8|_9|_10|_

There may be an overflow of feelings and thoughts; continue to journal when necessary.

DAY SEVENTEEN

Remember my preparation time and state my intention.

As I sit in the seat of my soul, I spiritually observe the impact I have had on siblings or the impact of being an only child. What type of positioning did I have to take with my siblings or as an only child to survive? How has that carried me through life? How has it hampered me or benefited my well-being? Are there any feelings of betrayals, resentments, jealousies, vindictive or cunning natures, sadness, rivalry, competitive spirits, anger, or pain that is controlling me as an adult? What behaviors do I use to survive?

Be honest and forthright with myself. Journal:

Which boundaries were dishonored, disrespected, violated, and compromised?

How have my emotions and behavior impacted my true power? Assess where my true power is on a scale of 1 to 10.

Power scale 1|_2|_3|_4|_5|_6|_7|_8|_9|_10|_

Journal:

Who shall be forgiven? I *intentionally* forgive _____.

Journal:

What am I feeling right now?

Establish boundaries.

I clarified and established my boundaries, which are _____.

I appreciate myself today because _____.

Pray a prayer of thanksgiving and end, while looking into the mirror, with the words: "I have *intentionally* forgiven myself, and my boundaries are _____ _____.

Peace ... peace ... peace."

Reassess my true power.

Power scale 1|_2|_3|_4|_5|_6|_7|_8|_9|_10|_

There may be an overflow of feelings and thoughts; continue to journal when necessary.

DAY EIGHTEEN

Remember my preparation time and state my intention.

As I sit in the seat of my soul, I spiritually observe my emotions and memories as I recap the last seventeen days of *intentional* forgiveness. What brought up fear, sadness, grief, and relief? What have I confronted that has been lifted from my spirit? What is lingering in my soul that feels unfinished and incomplete?

Be honest and forthright with myself. Journal:

Which boundaries were dishonored, disrespected, violated, and compromised?

How have my emotions and behavior impacted my true power? Assess where my true power is on a scale of 1 to 10.

Power scale 1|_2|_3|_4|_5|_6|_7|_8|_9|_10|_

Journal:

Who shall be forgiven? I *intentionally* forgive _____.

Journal:

What am I feeling right now?

Establish boundaries.

I clarified and established my boundaries, which are _____.

I appreciate myself today because, _____,

Pray a prayer of thanksgiving and end, while looking into the mirror, with the words: "I have *intentionally* forgiven myself, and my boundaries are _____

_____.

Peace ... peace ... peace."

Reassess my true power.

Power scale 1|_2|_3|_4|_5|_6|_7|_8|_9|_10|_

There may be an overflow of feelings and thoughts; continue to journal when necessary.

DAY NINETEEN

Remember my preparation time and state my intention.

As I sit in the seat of my soul, I spiritually observe my emotions and memories of my education experiences. Did I attend conventional educational institutions or not? What were my profound learning moments inside or outside of the educational institutions? How have the overall educational environments impacted me as an adult? What were good, bad, and indifferent experiences and memories?

Be honest and forthright with myself. Journal:

Which boundaries were dishonored, disrespected, violated, and compromised?

How have my emotions and behavior impacted my true power? Where is my true power on a scale of 1 to 10?

Power scale 1|_2|_3|_4|_5|_6|_7|_8|_9|_10|_

Journal:

Who shall be forgiven? I *intentionally* forgive _____.

Journal:

What am I feeling right now?

Establish boundaries.

I clarified and established my boundaries, which are _____,

I appreciate myself today because, _____.

Pray a prayer of thanksgiving and end, while looking into the mirror, with the words: "I have *intentionally* forgiven myself, and my boundaries are _____

_____.

Peace ... peace ... peace."

Reassess my true power.

Power scale 1|_2|_3|_4|_5|_6|_7|_8|_9|_10|_

There may be an overflow of feelings and thoughts; continue to journal when necessary.

DAY TWENTY

Remember my preparation time and state my intention.

As I sit in the seat of my soul, I spiritually observe my emotions and memories of my educational environments. Who were my friends? Did I feel included by my classmates/schoolmates and neighbors? Did I include my classmates/schoolmates and neighbors in my activities? What were the hardships and barriers of being in or not being in school?

Be honest and forthright with myself. Journal:

Which boundaries were dishonored, disrespected, violated, and compromised?

How have my emotions and memories of school impact my true power? Assess where my true power is on a scale of 1 to 10.

Power scale 1|_2|_3|_4|_5|_6|_7|_8|_9|_10|_

Journal:

Who shall be forgiven? I *intentionally* forgive _____.

Journal:

What am I feeling right now?

Establish boundaries.

I clarified and established my boundaries, which are _____,

I appreciate myself today because, _____,

Pray a prayer of thanksgiving and end, while looking into the mirror, with the words: "I have *intentionally* forgiven myself, and my boundaries are _____

_____,

Peace ... peace ... peace."

Reassess my true power.

Power scale 1|_2|_3|_4|_5|_6|_7|_8|_9|_10|_

There may be an overflow of feelings and thoughts; continue to journal when necessary.

DAY TWENTY-ONE

Remember my preparation time and state my intention.

As I sit in the seat of my soul, I spiritually observe my emotions and memories of the educational environments. What was my personality as a conventional student or not as a conventional student? Was I an impressionable or precocious student of school and or student of the streets? What were my fears about being in or not being in school? Did I feel safe and protected? Who did I trust inside or outside of school(s)? Was I ever betrayed? How did I negotiate my way through the school and street cultures?

Be honest and forthright with myself. Journal:

Which boundaries were dishonored, disrespected, violated, and compromised?

How have my emotions and memories impacted my true power? Assess where my true power is on a scale of 1 to 10.

Power scale 1|_2|_3|_4|_5|_6|_7|_8|_9|_10|_

Journal:

Who shall be forgiven? I *intentionally* forgive _____,

Journal:

What am I feeling right now?

Establish boundaries.

I clarified and established my boundaries, which are _____,

I appreciate myself today because _____,

Pray a prayer of thanksgiving and end, while looking into the mirror, with the words: "I have *intentionally* forgiven myself, and my boundaries are _____

_____,

Peace ... peace ... peace."

Reassess my true power.

Power scale 1|_2|_3|_4|_5|_6|_7|_8|_9|_10|_

There may be an overflow of feelings and thoughts; continue to journal when necessary.

DAY TWENTY-TWO

Remember my preparation time and state my intention.

As I sit in the seat of my soul, I spiritually observe my emotions and memories of my educational environments. How did my instructors, teachers, classmates, and schoolmates and or the street cultures influence my choices as an adult? What am I not proud of? What might I be ashamed of, not pleased with, and/or holding onto any bitterness, shame, blame, resentment, jealousies, and guilt? Are there any learned belief systems and dogma(s) that I held onto which are affecting my life that I cannot let go of?

Be honest and forthright with myself. Journal:

Which boundaries were dishonored, disrespected, violated, and compromised?

How have my emotions and memories impacted my true power? Assess where my true power is on a scale of 1 to 10.

Power scale 1|_2|_3|_4|_5|_6|_7|_8|_9|_10|_

Journal:

Who shall be forgiven? I *intentionally* forgive _____.

Journal:

What am I feeling right now?

Establish boundaries.

I clarified and established my boundaries, which are _____,

I appreciate myself today because, _____,

Pray a prayer of thanksgiving and end, while looking into the mirror, with the words: "I have *intentionally* forgiven myself, and my boundaries are _____ _____,

Peace ... peace ... peace."

Reassess my true power.

Power scale 1|_2|_3|_4|_5|_6|_7|_8|_9|_10|_

There may be an overflow of feelings and thoughts; continue to journal when necessary.

DAY TWENTY-THREE

Remember my preparation time and state my intention.

As I sit in the seat of my soul, I spiritually observe my emotions, feelings, and memories of educational institutions that I did not attend. What were my judgments about them? Did I desire to be a part of them or not? What did I think about the students/instructors of these educational institutions? What were my biases, prejudices, resentments, fears, longings? Why?

Be honest and forthright with myself. Journal:

Which boundaries were dishonored, disrespected, violated, and compromised?

How have my emotions and behavior impacted my true power? Where is my true power on a scale of 1 to 10?

Power scale 1|_2|_3|_4|_5|_6|_7|_8|_9|_10|_

Journal:

Who shall be forgiven? I *intentionally* forgive _____,

Journal:

What am I feeling right now?

Establish boundaries.

I clarified and established my boundaries, which are _____,

I appreciate myself today because _____,

Pray a prayer of thanksgiving and end, while looking into the mirror, with the words: "I have *intentionally* forgiven myself, and my boundaries are _____ _____

Peace ... peace ... peace."

Reassess my true power.

Power scale 1|_2|_3|_4|_5|_6|_7|_8|_9|_10|_

There may be an overflow of feelings and thoughts; continue to journal when necessary.

DAY TWENTY-FOUR

Remember my preparation time and state my intention.

As I sit in the seat of my soul, I spiritually observe my intimate relationships, and I pause in retrospect of my time with the men/women whom I have had relationships with and seek to know the unresolved issues with them. Was my time well spent with them? What were the missteps, hidden agendas, and benefits for being in relationship with them? Are there hidden and obvious anger, disappointments, shame, bitterness, embarrassment, and sadness?

Be honest and forthright with myself. Journal:

Which boundaries were dishonored, disrespected, violated, and compromised?

How have my emotions and behavior impacted my true power? Where is my true power on a scale of 1 to 10?

Power scale 1|_2|_3|_4|_5|_6|_7|_8|_9|_10|_

Journal:

Who shall be forgiven? I *intentionally* forgive _____.

Journal:

What am I feeling right now?

Establish boundaries.

I clarified and established my boundaries, which are _____.

I appreciate myself today because _____.

Pray a prayer of thanksgiving and end, while looking into the mirror, with the words: "I have *intentionally* forgiven myself, and my boundaries are _____

_____.

Peace ... peace ... peace."

Reassess my true power.

Power scale 1|_2|_3|_4|_5|_6|_7|_8|_9|_10|_

There may be an overflow of feelings and thoughts; continue to journal when necessary.

DAY TWENTY-FIVE

Remember my preparation time and state my intention.

As I sit in the seat of my soul, I spiritually observe my temperament about my intimate relationships. Who do I still hold onto from my childhood, adolescence, teenage years and adult hood? What about him/her is worth holding onto and why? Do they owe me something? Are they emotionally healthy for me?

Be honest and forthright with myself. Journal:

Which boundaries were dishonored, disrespected, violated, and compromised?

How have my emotions and behavior impacted my true power? Where is my true power on a scale of 1 to 10?

Power scale 1|_2|_3|_4|_5|_6|_7|_8|_9|_10|_

Journal:

Who shall be forgiven? I *intentionally* forgive _____.

Journal:

What am I feeling right now?

Establish boundaries.

I clarified and established my boundaries, which are _____,

I appreciate myself today because _____,

Pray a prayer of thanksgiving and end, while looking into the mirror, with the words: "I have *intentionally* forgiven myself, and my boundaries are _____ _____,

Peace ... peace ... peace."

Reassess my true power.

Power scale 1|_2|_3|_4|_5|_6|_7|_8|_9|_10|_

There may be an overflow of feelings and thoughts; continue to journal when necessary.

DAY TWENTY-SIX

Remember my preparation time and state my intention.

As I sit in the seat of my soul, I spiritually observe my emotions and feelings of my current intimate adult relationships. Are there needs, desires, and purposes for having them? Are there any manipulations, deceptions, compromises, misrepresentations, fears, and/or a want to be needed? Who am I pleasing by being in these intimate adult relationships? Are they healthy for me?

Be honest and forthright with myself. Journal:

Which boundaries were dishonored, disrespected, violated, and compromised?

How have my emotions and behavior impacted my true power? Where is my true power on a scale of 1 to 10?

Power scale 1|_2|_3|_4|_5|_6|_7|_8|_9|_10|_

Journal:

Who shall be forgiven? I *intentionally* forgive _____.

Journal:

What am I feeling right now?

Establish boundaries.

I clarified and established my boundaries, which are _____.

I appreciate myself today because _____.

Pray a prayer of thanksgiving and end, while looking into the mirror, with the words: "I have *intentionally* forgiven myself, and my boundaries are _____

_____.

Peace ... peace ... peace."

Reassess my true power.

Power scale 1|_2|_3|_4|_5|_6|_7|_8|_9|_10|_

There may be an overflow of feelings and thoughts; continue to journal when necessary.

DAY TWENTY-SEVEN

Remember my preparation time and state my intention.

As I sit in the seat of my soul, I spiritually observe my decision to become a parent or not to become a parent. Why did I decide to become or not become a parent? Do I appreciate being a parent or not being a parent? Are there any regrets, hardships, fears, disappointments? Did I miss out on anything ... any experience? Did I want to go in another direction? Why didn't I?

Be honest and forthright with myself. Journal:

Which boundaries were dishonored, disrespected, violated, and compromised?

How have my emotions and behavior impacted my true power? Where is my true power on a scale of 1 to 10?

Power scale 1|_2|_3|_4|_5|_6|_7|_8|_9|_10|_

Journal:

Who shall be forgiven? I *intentionally* forgive _____.

Journal:

What am I feeling right now?

Establish boundaries.

I clarified and established my boundaries, which are _____,

I appreciate myself today because _____,

Pray a prayer of thanksgiving and end, while looking into the mirror, with the words: "I have *intentionally* forgiven myself, and my boundaries are _____

_____

Peace ... peace ... peace."

Reassess my true power.

Power scale 1|_2|_3|_4|_5|_6|_7|_8|_9|_10|_

There may be an overflow of feelings and thoughts; continue to journal when necessary.

DAY TWENTY-EIGHT

Remember my preparation time and state my intention.

As I sit in the seat of my soul, I spiritually observe the sensitivity around parenthood. Were there any losses (as a parent or not being a parent) physically, emotionally, and mentally? How do I feel about the losses? What have I shared or not about the losses? How have the losses impacted my life?

Be honest and forthright with myself. Journal:

Which boundaries were dishonored, disrespected, violated, and compromised?

How have my emotions and behavior impacted my true power? Where is my true power on a scale of 1 to 10?

Power scale 1|_2|_3|_4|_5|_6|_7|_8|_9|_10|_

Journal:

Who shall be forgiven? I *intentionally* forgive _____.

Journal:

What am I feeling right now?

Establish boundaries.

I clarified and established my boundaries, which are _____.

I appreciate myself today because _____.

Pray a prayer of thanksgiving and end, while looking into the mirror, with the words: "I have *intentionally* forgiven myself, and my boundaries are _____

_____.

Peace ... peace ... peace."

Reassess my true power.

Power scale 1|_2|_3|_4|_5|_6|_7|_8|_9|_10|_

There may be an overflow of feelings and thoughts; continue to journal when necessary.

DAY TWENTY-NINE

Remember my preparation time and state my intention.

As I sit in the seat of my soul, I spiritually observe my feelings of the last twenty-eight days. Are there any vestiges of unforgiveness left in me of myself and all of the other relationships – family, friends, and enemies?

Be honest and forthright with myself. Journal:

Which boundaries were dishonored, disrespected, violated, and compromised?

How have my emotions and behavior impacted my true power? Where is my true power on a scale of 1 to 10?

Power scale 1|_2|_3|_4|_5|_6|_7|_8|_9|_10|_

Journal:

Who shall be forgiven? I *intentionally* forgive _____.

Journal:

What am I feeling right now?

Establish boundaries.

I clarified and established my boundaries, which are _____.

I appreciate myself today because _____.

Pray a prayer of thanksgiving and end, while looking into the mirror, with the words: "I have *intentionally* forgiven myself, and my boundaries are _____

_____

Peace ... peace ... peace."

Reassess my true power.

Power scale 1|_2|_3|_4|_5|_6|_7|_8|_9|_10|_

There may be an overflow of feelings and thoughts; continue to journal when necessary.

DAY THIRTY

Remember my preparation time and state my intention.

As I sit in the seat of my soul, I spiritually observe my feelings and judgments about social institutions. What is in my heart about social institutions? What are the institutionalized behaviors and habits of them, and how have these behaviors and habits impacted my life? What has been my role to improve or perpetuate any wrong, divisiveness, separations, prejudices, and biases that—or if—I may feel about social institutions? How do I feel about others who speak harshly about social institutions? What has been/is my experience with the social institutions?

Be honest and forthright with myself. Journal:

Which boundaries were dishonored, disrespected, violated, and compromised?

How have my emotions and behavior impacted my true power? Where is my true power on a scale of 1 to 10?

Power scale 1|_2|_3|_4|_5|_6|_7|_8|_9|_10|_

Journal:

Who shall be forgiven? I *intentionally* forgive _____.

Journal:

What am I feeling right now?

Establish boundaries.

I clarified and established my boundaries, which are _____.

I appreciate myself today because _____.

Pray a prayer of thanksgiving and end, while looking into the mirror, with the words: "I have *intentionally* forgiven myself, and my boundaries are _____ _____.

Peace … peace … peace."

Reassess my true power.

Power scale 1|_2|_3|_4|_5|_6|_7|_8|_9|_10|_

There may be an overflow of feelings and thoughts; continue to journal when necessary.

DAY THIRTY-ONE

Remember my preparation time and state my intention.

As I sit in the seat of my soul, I spiritually observe my emotions about the tragedies in the world. Who do I blame for the terrorists' attacks? Why do I blame them? How have the attacks impacted my behavior towards other people and myself? And, what is my part in these attacks? What have I perpetuated?

Be honest and forthright with myself. Journal:

Which boundaries were dishonored, disrespected, violated, and compromised?

How have my emotions and behavior impacted my true power? Where is my true power on a scale of 1 to 10?

Power scale 1|_2|_3|_4|_5|_6|_7|_8|_9|_10|_

Journal:

Who shall be forgiven? I *intentionally* forgive _____,

Journal:

What am I feeling right now?

Establish boundaries.

I clarified and established my boundaries, which are _____,

I appreciate myself today because _____,

Pray a prayer of thanksgiving and end, while looking into the mirror, with the words: "I have *intentionally* forgiven myself, and my boundaries are _____

_____,

Peace ... peace ... peace."

Reassess my true power.

Power scale 1|_2|_3|_4|_5|_6|_7|_8|_9|_10|_

There may be an overflow of feelings and thoughts; continue to journal when necessary.

DAY THIRTY-TWO

Remember my preparation time and state my intention.

As I sit in the seat of my soul, I spiritually observe my feelings about my national government agencies.

How do I feel about the regulatory and governing agencies in my country? What are my likes and dislikes about the implementations of the policies? Do I feel intimidated, manipulated, dismissed, afraid, betrayed, disappointed, invisible, unprotected, and powerless? Are these institutions life threatening to me? How have I been affected by these agencies?

Be honest and forthright with myself. Journal:

Which boundaries were dishonored, disrespected, violated, and compromised?

How have my emotions and behavior impacted my true power? Where is my true power on a scale of 1 to 10?

Power scale 1|_2|_3|_4|_5|_6|_7|_8|_9|_10|_

Journal:

Who shall be forgiven? I *intentionally* forgive _____.

Journal:

What am I feeling right now?

Establish boundaries.

I clarified and established my boundaries, which are _____.

I appreciate myself today because, _____.

Pray a prayer of thanksgiving and end, while looking into the mirror, with the words: "I have *intentionally* forgiven myself, and my boundaries are _____

_____.

Peace ... peace ... peace."

Reassess my true power.

Power scale 1|_2|_3|_4|_5|_6|_7|_8|_9|_10|_

There may be an overflow of feelings and thoughts; continue to journal when necessary.

DAY THIRTY-THREE

Remember my preparation time and state my intention.

As I sit in the seat of my soul, I spiritually observe my feelings as a global citizen and think about the wars – The Civil Wars, World War I, World War II, Korean War, Vietnam War, Conflicts in the Middle East, Desert Storm, Afghanistan, Iraq, Israel and Palestine, North Korea, Russia, Africa, ethnic cleansings, Latin America, Australia...(Pick at least one area) Who is to blame? How do I feel about the state of affairs in this world? What do I obsess about? What is my role, and am I in control of my destiny?

Be honest and forthright with myself. Journal:

Which boundaries were dishonored, disrespected, violated, and compromised?

How have my emotions and behavior impacted my true power? Where is my true power on a scale of 1 to 10?

Power scale 1|_2|_3|_4|_5|_6|_7|_8|_9|_10|_

Journal:

Who shall be forgiven? I *intentionally* forgive _____.

Journal:

What am I feeling right now?

Establish boundaries.

I clarified and established my boundaries, which are _____.

I appreciate myself today because _____.

Pray a prayer of thanksgiving and end, while looking into the mirror, with the words: "I have *intentionally* forgiven myself, and my boundaries are _____

_____.

Peace ... peace ... peace."

Reassess my true power.

Power scale 1|_2|_3|_4|_5|_6|_7|_8|_9|_10|_

There may be an overflow of feelings and thoughts; continue to journal when necessary.

DAY THIRTY-FOUR

Remember my preparation time and state my intention.

As I sit in the seat of my soul, I spiritually observe my health as I call out any and all wounds of unforgiveness in my emotions that have affected my health such as betrayals, rejections, deceptions, lies, etc. by family, friends and enemies. What am I holding in my heart?

Be honest and forthright with myself. Journal:

Which boundaries were dishonored, disrespected, violated, and compromised?

How have my emotions and behavior impacted my true power? Where is my true power on a scale of 1 to 10?

Power scale 1|_2|_3|_4|_5|_6|_7|_8|_9|_10|_

Journal:

Who shall be forgiven? I *intentionally* forgive _____.

Journal:

What am I feeling right now?

Establish boundaries.

I clarified and established my boundaries, which are _____.

I appreciate myself today because _____.

Pray a prayer of thanksgiving and end, while looking into the mirror, with the words: "I have *intentionally* forgiven myself, and my boundaries are _____

_____.

Peace ... peace ... peace."

Reassess my true power.

Power scale 1|_2|_3|_4|_5|_6|_7|_8|_9|_10|_

There may be an overflow of feelings and thoughts; continue to journal when necessary.

DAY THIRTY-FIVE

Remember my preparation time and state my intention.

As I sit in the seat of my soul, I spiritually observe my health on a cellular level, and, I call out for healing all unforgiveness' in my six senses: touch, taste, sight, smell, hearing and intuition. I ask myself what and or who is it that I don't want to touch or be touched by; taste or be tasted by; see or be seen by; smell or be smelled by; hear or be heard by; intuit or have my intuition sensed by? What am I avoiding to confront through any or all of my senses that will free me? What pain, grief, losses, hidden secrets, fears, etc., am I resisting to feel through my senses? What pleasures am I denying and depriving myself of? What am I holding in my heart?

Be honest and forthright with myself. Journal:

Which boundaries were dishonored, disrespected, violated, and compromised?

How have my emotions and behavior impacted my true power? Where is my true power on a scale of 1 to 10?

Power scale 1|_2|_3|_4|_5|_6|_7|_8|_9|_10|_

Journal:

Who shall be forgiven? I *intentionally* forgive _____.

Journal:

What am I feeling right now?

Establish boundaries.

I clarified and established my boundaries, which are _____.

I appreciate myself today because _____.

Pray a prayer of thanksgiving and end, while looking into the mirror, with the words: "I have *intentionally* forgiven myself, and my boundaries are _____ _____.

Peace ... peace ... peace."

Reassess my true power.

Power scale 1|_2|_3|_4|_5|_6|_7|_8|_9|_10|_

There may be an overflow of feelings and thoughts; continue to journal when necessary.

DAY THIRTY-SIX

Remember my preparation time and state my intention.

As I sit in the seat of my soul, I spiritually observe my health on a cellular level, and I recall when I have not listened to my intuition. Why did I not listen to my intuition? What were the consequences? What have I ignored? What have I learned from not listening? What pleasures am I avoiding?

Be honest and forthright with myself. Journal:

Which boundaries were dishonored, disrespected, violated, and compromised?

How have my emotions and behavior impacted my true power? Where is my true power on a scale of 1 to 10?

$$\text{Power scale } 1|\_2|\_3|\_4|\_5|\_6|\_7|\_8|\_9|\_10|\_$$

Journal:

Who shall be forgiven? I *intentionally* forgive _____.

Journal:

What am I feeling right now?

Establish boundaries.

I clarified and established my boundaries, which are _____.

I appreciate myself today because _____.

Pray a prayer of thanksgiving and end, while looking into the mirror, with the words: "I have *intentionally* forgiven myself, and my boundaries are _____

_____.

Peace ... peace ... peace."

Reassess my true power.

$$\text{Power scale } 1|\_2|\_3|\_4|\_5|\_6|\_7|\_8|\_9|\_10|\_$$

There may be an overflow of feelings and thoughts; continue to journal when necessary.

DAY THIRTY-SEVEN

Remember my preparation time and state my intention.

As I sit in the seat of my soul, I spiritually observe my current financial state. Do I have the assets that I desire? How have I managed my money, and am I earning the income that reflects who I am? Am I happy and satisfied with my earnings? What, if needed, can I do to improve my income status? What belief system, if any, is holding me back? When I don't have money, how do I feel about myself?

Be honest and forthright with myself. Journal:

Which boundaries were dishonored, disrespected, violated, and compromised?

How have my emotions and behavior impacted my true power? Where is my true power on a scale of 1 to 10?

Power scale 1|_2|_3|_4|_5|_6|_7|_8|_9|_10|_

Journal:

Who shall be forgiven? I *intentionally* forgive _____.

Journal:

What am I feeling right now?

Establish boundaries.

I clarified and established my boundaries, which are _____,

I appreciate myself today because _____,

Pray a prayer of thanksgiving and end, while looking into the mirror, with the words: "I have *intentionally* forgiven myself, and my boundaries are _____

_____.

Peace ... peace ... peace."

Reassess my true power.

Power scale 1|_2|_3|_4|_5|_6|_7|_8|_9|_10|_

There may be an overflow of feelings and thoughts; continue to journal when necessary.

DAY THIRTY-EIGHT

Remember my preparation time and state my intention.

As I sit in the seat of my soul, I spiritually observe my relationship with money. What is more important: money or me? Can I exist without money? Which is which ... does money make me, or do I make money? Do I obsess about money? Do I run after money? In what ways have I compromised my dreams and desires to acquire money? How do I acquire money to take care of myself? Have I compromised relationships or have I been compromised by others about money matters?

Be honest and forthright with myself. Journal:

Which boundaries were dishonored, disrespected, violated, and compromised?

How have my emotions and behavior impacted my true power? Where is my true power on a scale of 1 to 10?

Power scale 1|_2|_3|_4|_5|_6|_7|_8|_9|_10|_

Journal:

Who shall be forgiven? I *intentionally* forgive _____.

Journal:

What am I feeling right now?

Establish boundaries.

I clarified and established my boundaries, which are _____.

I appreciate myself today because _____.

Pray a prayer of thanksgiving and end, while looking into the mirror, with the words: "I have *intentionally* forgiven myself, and my boundaries are _____

_____.

Peace ... peace ... peace."

Reassess my true power.

Power scale 1|_2|_3|_4|_5|_6|_7|_8|_9|_10|_

There may be an overflow of feelings and thoughts; continue to journal when necessary.

DAY THIRTY-NINE

Remember my preparation time and state my intention.

As I sit in the seat of my soul, I spiritually observe my relationship with myself. What have I given in to that did not reflect who I am? Are there any vestiges of unforgiveness left in me that need to be cleared out? Am I willing to let go of past missteps, actions, and behaviors that have caused me hurt, bitterness, resentment, vindictiveness, sorrow, guilt and shame, and feelings of grief and pain? It's my call ...

Be honest and forthright with myself. Journal:

Which boundaries were dishonored, disrespected, violated, and compromised?

How have my emotions and behavior impacted my true power? Where is my true power on a scale of 1 to 10?

Power scale 1|_2|_3|_4|_5|_6|_7|_8|_9|_10|_

Journal:

Who shall be forgiven? I *intentionally* forgive _____ .

Journal:

What am I feeling right now?

Establish boundaries.

I clarified and established my boundaries, which are _____ .

I appreciate myself today because _____ .

Pray a prayer of thanksgiving and end, while looking into the mirror, with the words: "I have *intentionally* forgiven myself, and my boundaries are _____

_____ .

Peace ... peace ... peace."

Reassess my true power.

Power scale 1|_2|_3|_4|_5|_6|_7|_8|_9|_10|_

There may be an overflow of feelings and thoughts; continue to journal when necessary.

DAY FORTY

Remember my preparation time and state my intention.

As I sit in the seat of my soul, I spiritually observe my feelings, and I ask myself, how many ways do I love myself? What keeps me going? What am I holding back? Who is in charge of my destiny? Can I trust and protect myself? What am I holding onto in my heart? Who/what is my secret lover? Who am I?

Be honest and forthright with myself. Journal:

Which boundaries were dishonored, disrespected, violated, and compromised?

How have my emotions and behavior impacted my true power? Where is my true power on a scale of 1 to 10?

Power scale 1|_2|_3|_4|_5|_6|_7|_8|_9|_10|_

Journal:

Who shall be forgiven? I *intentionally* forgive _____.

Journal:

What am I feeling right now?

Establish boundaries.

I clarified and established my boundaries, which are _____.

I appreciate myself today because _____.

Pray a prayer of thanksgiving and end, while looking into the mirror, with the words: "I have *intentionally* forgiven myself, and my boundaries are _____

_____.

Peace ... peace ... peace."

Reassess my true power.

Power scale 1|_2|_3|_4|_5|_6|_7|_8|_9|_10|_

There may be an overflow of feelings and thoughts; continue to journal when necessary.

Although the practice of forgiveness continues into infinitum, this is the completion of the 40-Day *Intentional* Forgiveness Practice. Remember to be kindhearted to yourself, and when you make a decision, be clear about why you are making it.

I appreciate you and I thank you. Peace and blessings. W. L. Watson Wilfong, R.Sc.P.

MY ASSESSMENT

What were/are my insights about my boundaries?

_____

_____

_____

_____

_____

What and who were major forgiveness' and why?

_____

_____

_____

_____

_____

What and who am I holding onto?

_____

_____

_____

_____

_____

Which forgiveness exercise(s) must I go over again?

_____

_____

_____

_____

_____

What must I pay attention to when I make life altering decisions?

_____

_____

_____

_____

_____

What do I appreciate about myself and am grateful for after these 40-days of intrapersonal reflections?

_____

_____

_____

_____

_____

MY GRATITUDE AND APPRECIATION LIST

_____   _____
_____   _____
_____   _____
_____   _____
_____   _____
_____   _____
_____   _____
_____   _____
_____   _____
_____   _____
_____   _____
_____   _____
_____   _____
_____   _____
_____   _____
_____   _____
_____   _____
_____   _____
_____   _____
_____   _____
_____   _____
_____   _____
_____   _____

LIFE IS OUR BEST FRIEND.

I speak into the hearts of everyone reading this prose. I declare life as our best friend. It shows up. It is always here for us. It loves us. It never forsakes us. It understands us. It is loving and forgiving. It continually provides for us everything that we need. It is the complete composition of elements: water, air, soil, fire, wood, and metal. It gives us the seasons. It gives us the earth, the sky, and above and below. It sustains us and maintains us. It is our best friend.

Life is whole and complete. It confronts and challenges us. It gives us the opportunity to grow and evolve into different states of beingness. It is the reflection of who we are. We are the sadness, the joy, the peace, the power, the fear, the tears, and the rich and the poor. We are the firmness and the tenderness. We are the good and the bad, the ugly and the beautiful.

We are the simplicity and complexity of ourselves. We are trusting and we are distrusting. We are our traitor and our beloved. We are our friend and our foe. We are the giver to and the taker from ourselves. We are our teacher and our student. We are our child and our parent. We are who we are and we are our best friend.

We are our best friend. We are the complete composition of ourselves. We are the precious gems of the earth. We are all that we need.

We are our best friend.

We are all of life. We come with everything that we need to:

-live. – laugh. – listen. – taste. – smell. – touch. – hear. – see. – sense. – forgive. – cry. – thrive. – love. – prosper. – We are our own best friend.

We commit to give ourselves the best of ourselves and to always seek to know more of who we are.

We are grateful and thankful for our lives for life is my best friend.

Live richly, live fully, live joyfully, live freely, live forgivingly, live well.

Ashe', Amen, Ashe'.

Sincerely I AM,

W. L. Watson Wilfong, R.Sc.P.
Contact information: forgivetoprosper@gmail.com

BIBLIOGRAPHY

The Holy Bible: From the Ancient Eastern Text. George M. Lamsa's Translation from the Aramaic of the Peshitta. San Francisco: Harper, 1933.

Holmes, Ernest. *Words That Heal Today.* New York: Dodd, Mead & Company, 1949 *A Course in Miracles,* Vol. 1. Tiburon: Foundation for Inner Peace, 1975.

SUGGESTED READINGS

A Course in Miracles. **Tiburon: Foundation for Inner Peace, 1975.**

Beckwith, Michael Bernard, *lifevisioning: A Four Stage Evolutionary Journey to Live as Divine Love,* **Louisville: Sounds True, 2008 (CDs)**

Beckwith, Michael Bernard, *Spiritual Liberation: Fulfilling Your Soul's Potential.* **Hillsboro: Beyond Words, 2008**

Eker, T. Harv, *Secrets of the Millionaire Mind: Mastering the Inner Game of Wealth.* **New York: HarperCollins, 2005.**

Ferrini, Paul, *The Laws of LOVE.* **Greenfield: HeartwaysPress, 2004.**

Franke, Ursula, *The River Never Looks Back: Historical and Practical Foundations of Bert Hellinger's Family Constellations.* **Carl-Auer-Systeme Verlag und Verlagsbuchhandlung GmbH, 2003.**

Healing spiritually: Renewing your life through the power of God's law. **Boston: The Christian Science Publishing Society, 1996.**

Hellinger, Bert, Gabriel Ten Hovel. *Acknowledging What Is: Conversation with Bert Hellinger.* **Zieg, Tucker, 1999.**

Holmes, Ernest, *The Science of Mind.* **New York: Dodd, Mead & Company, 1938.**

Holmes, Ernest, *Words that Heal Today.* **New York: Dodd, Mead & Company, 1975.**

Lamsa, George M., *Holy Bible From the Ancient Eastern Text.* **San Francisco: Harper, 1933.**

Mindell, Arnold, *THE DEEP DEMOCRACY OF OPEN FORUMS: How to Transform Organizations into Communities: Practical Steps To Conflict Prevention And Resolution For The Family,Workplace And World,* **Hampton Roads: 2002**

Mindell, Arnold, *Quantum Mind and Healing: How to Listen and Respond to Your Body's Symptoms.* **Hampton Roads: 2004.**

Price, John Randolph, *The Abundance Book.* **Carlsbad: Hay House, Inc., 1996.**

Rollins, J.K., *Harry Potter and the Sorcerer's Stone.* **Scholastic Paperbacks: 1999.**

Tumpkin, Rev.Mary, *Before You Pray, Forgive.* **St. Anne: Universal Truth, 1998.**

Vanzant, Iyanla, *Peace from Broken Pieces*: *How to Get Through What You're Going Through.* New York: Hay House, Inc., 2010.

Watts, Marie S., *Just Be Yourself.* San Gabriel: Willing Publishing Company, 1972.

ABOUT THE AUTHOR

Wyllene (W. L. Watson Wilfong), born into a Catholic family in the United States, had the desire to live overseas and pursue a career in fashion design. She became pregnant at an early age and then knew that something in her soul was fundamentally altered. She became a seeker to regain her desires of fashion design but was never on target. In 1992, she was licensed as a spiritual counselor and kept pursuing the freedom which was fundamentally altered as a teenager. Wyllene participated as a team facilitator with the Process Oriented Psychology Organization of Portland, Oregon to bring awareness to unconscious behavior patterns and how to heal and enrich personal and group relationships. Wyllene founded, Acts of Power, a transformational training organization that developed and implemented a program to assist Afrikan Americans with ways to unravel the systemic behavior of oppression.

She trained in Family Constellations, developed by Bert Hellinger, to learn and apply the experiential methods that detect the interruption of the natural soul process; and, brings to consciousness why an individual maybe stuck in achieving healthy relationships, healthy finances, healthy health, a satisfying career and a solid spiritual foundation - total wellbeing.

Wyllene realized that from all of the forums she participated in, forgiveness was the key for her. She became aware that she had a sound pack with God and that the love of God is so unmovable, unwavering and unshakable that no matter what choices she made in the past that the love of God kept her spirit in tack, always. She had to understand that even though God loved her, she had to have the same unwavering, unmovable, unshakable love for herself; and, by actively taking account of her past, shucking off the energy of old negative beliefs, making amends with herself, and getting resolve, Wyllene became free; and, she knows that to maintain the freedom, forgiveness is an ongoing practice. Thus, she writes this workbook of *intentional* forgiveness trusting that it will serve to heal many who are in emotional bondage by resentment, blame, shame, guilt, self destructive behavior; and, it will assist in uncovering unidentifiable pain and anger.

Wyllene lives an eclectic lifestyle. She has a spiritual practice, is the administrator of a national trade association and an independent energy consultant. Traveling, street bazaars, and celebrating family and friends, writing inspirational messages, eating fun and different types of foods, renovation of properties, listening to soul stirring music of different genres and taking walks by the water are her passions.

Wyllene has a BS degree in Social Science, lives in the Southern United States, is married, has two adult sons and is MiMi to Rashid, Janiya and Josiah and is Mah! Lene to Brooklynne R.

Wyllene's motto is *"Helping Others to Thrive"*.

JOURNAL

JOURNAL

JOURNAL

JOURNAL

JOURNAL

JOURNAL

JOURNAL

JOURNAL

JOURNAL

JOURNAL

JOURNAL

JOURNAL

JOURNAL

JOURNAL

JOURNAL

JOURNAL